Postcards from the
Line of Demarcation
Points of Separation in Poetic Prose

by Branch Isole

Mana'o Publishing
P O Box 1696
Lahaina, HI 96767-1696

My poetry is inspired by the Hula.
The Hula is precise, sensual, sexual
and sophisticatedly raw as it tells a story.
I am a voyeur of the Hula for all its character.

The poems herein are short stories of
issues and emotions surrounding personal
responsibility choice and avoidance.
This is 'Voyeurism Poetry'.

Postcards from the Line of Demarcation
contains adult material and language,
some of which is sexual in nature.
It is intended for mature audiences only.

Contents

Introduction

At various times in our lives we arrive
at precipice points whether by requirement or
choice and we look over the edge of our
existence.   When this Line of Demarcation
become self evident, we are faced with our
mortality, morality and soul filling humanity.
How we respond in that moment of decision
determines not only who we are, but who we
will become in the next moment and in all those
to follow.

These fifty two 'Postcards' are for those
who choose to look beyond the surface images.

Branch Isole

Real poetry doesn't say anything
It just ticks off the possibilities
Opens all doors.

~Jim Morrison

Ainokea

God's spoken words
in declaration of His universal sovereignty
for all to hear and understand
were contained in His statement
"I am who I am"

Satan,
that fallen angel
unable to take
God's Holy place
was cast to earth
to plague and lead astray
this whole human race

With temptations, deceit, lies
and sin
his job each day
souls to win
Gathering to his side
all who might into the abyss
that they may with him abide

Interesting isn't it
after all these years
the one who has caused
so many tears
Satan, that old deceiver
has a stronghold grasp
on so many believers

Satan has tried
to be as God from the start
and his success is in
plying man's heart
Twisting God's own sovereign words
"I am"

That's not however
what Satan declares
as he watches and waits
on man's despair

The devil's no fool
inviting many
to be drawn to him
and his evil ways
By planting seeds
within the common
woman or man
who truly think
it's all about them

You see it
over and over again
in our behavior
our actions
our irresponsibility
Multitudes worldwide
openly declare
"It's all about me"

How has Satan
circumvented his place
and condemned those of us
in this human race
who state daily a plethora
of our self purposed Ainokea?

God exclaimed
"I am, I am"
Satan has taught us
to proudly proclaim
"*It*'s *a*bout *me*"
"*It*'s *a*bout *me*"
(I am I am)

[Ainokea (pronounced, Eye No Key Ah)
Hawaiian connotation for
'It's all about me'
literal meaning; "I do what I like"
"I do what I want"]

At Long Last My Love

Come my love
let me show you the wonders
Come my love
let the world not asunder,
our love nor our lives
'neath the clear or the thunder

For my love reaches above
beyond and forever
You I shall love now and then
leaving you never

It is you my love
whom God has sent
It is you my love
for whom I rent
all veils of the world
all decisions
temptations,
I give up them all
for the love of two

Him and you
you and He,
The two of you.

for CC

Awareness

You are
You are not
You want to be

Choices abound
within these three

You're a cook
a chaplain
a candlestick maker
The number one chief
janitor, tailor or baker

If who you are
is what you do,
with each career change
is there a new you?
Or are you the same
while traversing each new
identity game?

Playing for time
disguised as who you are not,
or who you want to be
If you are not as projected
or as perceived
who is it you are,
not
attempting to be?

If you want to be different
from whom you have been
are,
or are not
That seedling is planted
deep within

In the soul
of every woman and man
Buried beneath layers
of reality's plan
Waits for each
a nurturing caress
Encouraging us
to be our worst,
our best
Daily,
in the time
each has left

You are
You are not
You want to be

It is up to you
to become aware
to discover, to see
the choices
which abound
within these three

Beauty, the Beast

If I can't be beauty
permit me be beast
by inking and piercing
my body at least
then I know
you'll look
you'll stare,
at me

instead of her

Birthing Partner

Visiting his birthing partner
one last time today
Dressed in her finest
she's finally gone away
Going home
he was told
Prepared for travel
brave and bold

Or was she?
He stared and wondered

Had she planned at all
for this day,
the day she'd be put
down and under

She never talked of it
Not to his knowledge,
not through grade school
high school or even college

Exclaimed she 'believed'
That was to be
her last word
on the 'Son of Man'
Now she'll be
finding out first hand

Bidding farewell
to his birthing partner
of oh so long ago
Until he too arrives postmortem
he will never know

Characterless

With each lie told
one's credibility erodes
and that's how it goes
for the liar

The liar wants us to think
he's been right to the brink,
to the edge
to the rim
through all thick and thin
Surviving calamity
of biblical scale
fended off malaise
by tooth and nail

Liars hope we'll share the vision
of their beleaguered state of affairs
Through our eyes
with them we'll agree
conspiratorially

Believing they escape skepticism
Enmeshed in a myriad of excuses
Listening ears quickly learn
their proffered false words
soon are discerned

Full of hot air
their toxicity runneth over
exuding a stench
from which we take cover
The truth is,
as with Peter and his Wolf
after a while
we simply don't care

Then wishes for that limerick
of childhood days come true
to see that 'liar liar
with pants on fire'

Immolation is terrible
and no one enjoys
the burning stake's flaming pyre
except,
when it happens
to the pathological liar

got a match?

for Sylvia and Jonathan

Children Live What They Learn
and Learn What They See

Life's lessons exist
for each generation to know
but when personally embroiled
ownership of each
strikes strictly solo

Time trials of tribulation
our children don't believe
the experiences they live,
for many their firsts
were part of their parents' pasts,
when they as fore-bearers
tested their worth

A parent's job
is to couch and to coach
Reflecting on mistakes
the ones recalled most
Advice to give
to their children they bade,
"Do as I say, not as I did"

But adolescent minds think
they know best
given all their years
of experience
So off they go
full speed ahead
unpreparedly preparing
to bury themselves
in newly made beds

When will they learn? . .
When will we?

Repeating mistakes
while expecting different results
is committing behavior insanity

Comatose

Unconscious indiscretions dance
as conscientious thoughts
within my conscience,
while my vegetative state
of comatose continues

No conscious exorcism necessary
For this unconscious state of possession
is invested not with the devil
nor infested by his minions
It is held tight
in the grasp of delusion
exhibiting itself blatantly
A signpost of hyper deficiency
in common sensibility
as I waft in and out
of its omnipresence

Fed and watered,
readied for slaughter
Peeping with mind's eye
over the horizon's ledge
through the fog, beyond the mist
straining to distinguish
those alive in my brain
and yet lost,
to the world of my reality

Familiar faces,
old haunts
and places
Near sighted images
cascade into view

Focus, refocus
behind closed eyes
that stutter
Blaming failure
on this,
on that
Acknowledging truth
haltingly told
behind lids that flutter

Reciting deceitful lines
long ago forgotten,
now remembered
Becoming the sole pathway to life,
the one mankind knows

Recurring refrains
stand as monoliths
while pieces and parts
of a disabled heart
are at once disarmed,
dismembered,
dismissed

Through each and every
shallow breath,
to the world outside
fallow evidence of death alive

Comes the Gray

Some say
From stress it comes
Others claim
From age it grows
The Book expresses wisdom its source
Still, no one really knows

Change it does
As the days themselves do
Almost indiscernibly
Without rhythm
rhyme or clue

We may say
we feel the same
perhaps a bit tired or worn,
but the truth shines
eventually through
from the first day we are born

From the moment of breath first taken
the process begins unabated
From the alpha to the omega
its life having been prior slated

Through both the long
and the short of it
The answer, few can say
Why
Why
Why,
Why we continue to gray?

From none
to salt and pepper,
fading to smudging gray
Next silver
Now white
Transforming its wearer
metamorphosis,
seemingly overnight

From shockingly brilliant
and flowing locks
to thinning hair
as age doth knock
upon the door
so tightly held closed,
Why we gray
no one knows.

Cyber Loss

Recalling the screen
Colored blank green
Waiting for black words
to be born on white
Watching for invisible letters
to appear in plain sight

Intently listening
to hear your silent voice
Fingers whispering
in the other room?
Holding my breath
Exchange of key phrases
Knowing unheard words
seal my doom!

Sounds of clicking
is all I discern
Fingers fly across a keyboard
secretly writing your new lover
soon am I spurned?

alive
dead,
right
or wrong,
wealthy
poor,
weak
or strong

who am I?
how to decide?
what am I to do?
stay here?
why am I trying so hard
to get back to you?

Days of Endearment

Nothing has changed
in the nature of man
except that he does,
when caught in the grip
of the devil's hand

We chase the dollar
three hundred, sixty five days a year
and set aside few
for our Lord endeared

None is willing
to close the door
Simply said,
all three want more

Deadly Sins

Proudly proclaiming
himself to be
a called man of God
His presentation that
of a charismatic bear
for he is enormously huggable,
like others
behind those vestments worn
his life too
a see-sawing struggle

His penchant;
money making schemes
ideas and thoughts abound
Built on the backs
of subservient others
those who are out and down
Believing him the way
in need of his, being around

A taste of the Word,
shelter,
essential needs be filled
but one of the roles
they acquiesce to
is that of recovering shill

His expectation in return
indentured service sans retreat
Masked as freedom
to help each of them
get back on their feet

Cars, trucks
expensive motorcycles,
to him they come and go
Passing through his hands;
houses, acreage, land
Material avarice veiled beneath
the banner of this Pied Piper's clan

Now I wouldn't really
call it sloth
it's more like too much stuff
When I asked him
why so much? His answer,
"when is enough enough?"

One of his flock
recently announced,
he has changed immensely
"He's more under control
a kinder, gentler fellow
whose anger has now subsided
For now if you decide
to take your leave
he won't kick you out
nor will you now be chided"

My wife happened to mention
his greeting hug one Sunday
felt to her more than friendly
"to say the least" she said to me
"his rub
rubbed me the wrong way"

Now I'm not one to throw those stones
be they big or small
for the house I live in is full of glass
inhabited by a sinner
But our portions differ in comparison
for breakfast, lunch and dinner
for between the two of us
I admit, being somewhat thinner

He called me just the other day
an offer for me to take
Thanking him for thinking of me
heartily I declined
For his offers most often mean
a payday for him
at the expense of the offeree

He said he'd heard
that we'd done well
proceeding to say his good bye
But something in his parting tone
gave a sense he wished
we'd go to. . .

well, you know.

Differentials

there are His poems
and there are my poems
the difference plain to see
His are about truth and love
mine are about mine and me

Expressly

Waiting on you Santa
to transport us back
to when we still believed
Looking now to these holidays
grant us your pure relief

Gifts for those held dear
important to us and loved
Asking expectantly
for goodwill guidance
to come from up above

With season's greeting shared
we take this solitary moment
to express how much we care

~ Happy Holidays

Eye Trolling

Once upon a time in America,
A tattooed and grungy
biker outlaw look
was itself enough to keep
any populace shook

Every self-respecting
Hog riding
original and wanna-be
sat straddled
parading on at least,
one-thousand cc's

Sole design and intent
to draw outrageous glares
as well as the occasional
quasi- appreciative stare

Slowing down
to the posted speed
at each corner and intersection
Insuring for on-lookers
either an exciting mental boner
or frightening cardiac infarction

That was then,
That was when,
Living for weekend strolling
Bikers gathered into groups
and across local landscapes
went rolling

Their mission simple
a few cherished moments
of awed recognition . .
An afternoon of identity
with a little local eye trolling

How ubiquitous
in this land of nod
Oh how those times have changed
Now every middle aged outlaw
out on his asphalt prowl
finds it necessary
to parade through town
slowed to a virtual crawl

Engines revved up
to maximum loud
Efforts to pry
all those coveted eyes
from those tattooed and insecure
now mingling with the crowd

No longer time
for drugs or sex
nor rock 'n roll revelry
At twenty first century
parade planning meets
all efforts are focused on,
How to compete?

For the eye-locked attentions
of those desired main street shoppers,
"the ones we need so desperately
to gawk at our choppers"

For Saturdays and Sundays
belong to us
and those are *our days*
to make a fuss
It's incumbent upon
originals as we
to now incorporate multi-sensory
To regain our rightful
place and rank
on the totem pole
of social insecurity
In order to guarantee
all street lookers are made aware
we're the ones
here being wronged
As we grasp and clutch
to our breasts, to our bosoms
the place where defiant looks and attitudes
truly belong

Never did these seniors think
in their wildest dreams,
of a day long off
which would arrive
when their thunder would be stolen
and their presence eclipsed, pushed aside
By tattooed and pierced
punks, geeks
and offensively weird
who in Toyotas, Nissans
and Kias ride

Fellowship of Believers Prayer

God in heaven
Maker of all things
Judge of all men
I acknowledge and bewail
my manifold sins and wickedness
against thee and thy divine majesty
in thought, word and deed
Have mercy on my soul

Grant that I may here ever after
walk in newness of life
and follow the light of the world
my Lord and Savior
Jesus Christ

Lord come dwell in my heart
for you know what it is
I wish to do
and that is to serve you
this day and all the days of my life

For you are the master
and I am the servant
You are the vine
and I am the branch
You are the potter
and I am the clay
May I abide in you
that you would abide in me
May I serve you by serving others
and serve others while serving you

May your spirit guide me
lead me
and direct me
to where you would have me be
That all I am might reflect of you
and all I do
might be good works in your name
bringing honor and glory to you and the Father

These things I ask and pray
in the name of Jesus Christ
the true son
of the living God

my Lord
my Savior
my Rock
my Redeemer
my Fortress
my Shield
my Strength and my God.
Amen

Grave Situation

Lord give us strength
to go on one more day
that we might serve you
in some small way

Give us our bread
in a world that lacks
Give us a way
in your name to give back

The world today
has troubles its own
except for those
who through them have grown

The choices we make
the seeds of our struggles be
The decisions we take
can set us free
The choices each
ours to make
The risks of deciding
ours to take

Do something
Do nothing
Do right
Do wrong
Moment by moment
Short life or long

Daily Choices, Decisions
of how we'll behave
follow or lead us
unto the grave

.

Heavy

Everything has weight,
even Airheads

Hello

When life became theater
and drama interposed,
self-centered idolatry
became inbred
with the advent of the cellular phone
Spreading negative energy worldwide
Exacerbating in nanoseconds
to every nation
tell-all telecom proliferation

Every solitary thought or action
has now become public talk fodder
Piling to the rafters
self-important exploits
transmitted in real time
or in moments immediately thereafter

Tales compiled
Stories composed
Commentaries and Critique
With added visuals making taller
the beehive of being,
The Caller

How Desperate Am I?

He lied to me
in my bed
He lied to me
when I gave him head
He lied to me
before and after
he had all my holes
but at least in front
of all his friends
he grins and calls me
his only 'Ho'

Gone for three months
I thought I knew
but alas, I didn't
he lied to her too
Returned to find
it was her he was doing
and all along
I believed
it was only me
he was screwing

He lied
He cheated
He went behind my back
but right from the start
he was my heart

I soon found out
everyone knew,
everyone of course except me
Even the soap man
can you believe?

It all worked out
as I hoped it would
For a few days after my return
she realized too
she'd been burned
Took her about four seconds
to kick him to the curb
Gosh, she must be
really disturbed

She said it was
honesty and integrity he lacked
Lucky for me, huh
'cuz I got him back

I know my heart
can't be trusted
he'll do it again
even if busted
I know my heart's love
is no more than a sham
but that goes to show,
how truly desperate I am

I Don't Need You God

I Don't Need You God
To guide my way
through the night
or the day
Upon this path
is your loving light
which I will follow
unto the last

I Don't Need You God
to talk to me
about your word
Believe me Lord
our quests are in reach
I'll learn, You Teach

I Don't Need You God
to be near
awaiting to be asked
You always dry every tear
when it's in your love we bask

I Don't Need You God
to take my hand
in order to better
understand
Your Word is the wisdom
which quenches life's thirst
extinguishes the fires
of ignorance

I Don't Need You God
I can do it all
on my own
As long as you walk with me
from here
to your throne

I Don't Need You God
except I do,
and each time I ask
petition or pray
you surround me
with you, night and day

My life is not
as we wanted it to be
but you've stayed the course
and from the beginning
it was I who wavered
stumbled
and fell
While you remained steadfast
my doubts to quell

Although you're always here
I know your blessing
for me oh Lord
is that you won't interfere

I Hate You Right Now

So, do you make faces
behind their backs
and mutter under your breath
all the things you're going to do?

Do you have conversations
in your head
for each lame excuse
they might use,
while your only response is
fuck you!

Do you punch the air
wishing it were their heads
your pummeling contact is with?

Do you refuse to talk
when in they walk
because you still don't know
what else to do
How far you're willing to go
on the path of 'being through'?

Well, what are you waiting for?
Say out loud what you really think
and perhaps you'll discover
where your responsibility begins and ends
in this relationship

If

Having sown
your future's reap
If you die
in your sleep
Do your thoughts awaken
before you die,
or after?

It's All Good

If "It's All Good"
then why every time
I hear it said
are you always
hanging your head,
as if you have just learned
you've been slighted?

Why is your tone
one of dejection,
your emotions singed
by the hint of rejection?

When you say
"It's All Good"
why does your demeanor project
a false self-assurance
as you inject,
"It doesn't matter"
while your body language screams
"It does!"

You respond,
"It's All Good"
but your attitude speaks volumes
as seething revenge
dangles its carrot of martyrdom
until your very essence
is totally consumed

If "It's All Good"
why the ever present
'short-end-of-the-stick' look
as if you've had something of value
which someone took

When queried
your anecdotal reply is
"It's All Good"
through and through,
but who exactly
are you trying to convince,
me,
or you?

Lesson Less

Temptation to turn away
one final time,
once again

How many occasions
of vacillation, rebellion
have there been?

Why do we go
back and forth
to and from
this temporal security place
In a repetitious state of falling
once again, from grace

Our human way
anticipation, expectation
according to plans all our own
Stilted and stiffed
by yesterday's 'no'
today's rejecting, no growth zone

Crawling back
a last resort
our pathway's terminal stop?
perhaps humbled
perhaps not

In reality
always more than embarrassed
facing shame's conquest
from prior remembrance

Neither old
nor new
lesson learned

Line Drawings

A line of demarcation
drawn between
comfortable
and comfortably numb
is not validated
by the number of times you say,
"I love you"

Masked in a mist
as vaporous as a veil of smoke
It's the tone
the attitude
the way,
your lack of commitment
comes blazing through

More important matters
grasp your attention
from what was once
us

Courting died
when the spark of infatuation was doused
and left to smolder
as you turned away

Your claim of
'being here'
rings clamorous
on occasion,
but are you?. . . Truly?

So you say,
as if expecting
I will believe you
this time
as with how many others before

Holding the key
to my freedom
clutched dearly
by your insecurity
Wondering,
to where
did that youthful dream fade
while morphing into your life

Having made myself
a prisoner
once vexed by 'love'
in order to open the door
Now serving
its false sibling,
Indifference

Loose Change

'A penny for your thoughts
He stated demurely'

"I suspect you want to put
your two cents in
adding to all the advice
prior given,
for my outrageous actions
and egregious sin"?

'I'm not sure my few words
would be worth a plug nickel'
he retorted with a grin

'I just thought
you might like to share
and thus, clear some air
Trade a little of that latent grief
for a moment's respite, relief'

"Well, simply put"
she began to lament
"I dropped a dime on my ex
and to jail he went"

"It made me feel
like a two bit scoundrel
but he and his thugs
put me to the test
Threatening
then boasting
in peace, I'd rest"

"We'll see how tough
he really is
in that cage upstate,
the one with the enormous
walls and gates"

"I had a life-changing decision to make
so I flipped a coin
one of two chances to take
Using my old man's
last Kennedy half dollar,
It came up tails
I called the cops
They made the collar"

"From behind those bars
he declared, made it clear
for six bits
he'd have me shot,
gunned down
without a thought,
if I didn't lie
when I testified"

"He threatened,
promising harm
and now I've had enough"

"Just like him
I'll make it clear
I refuse to be bullied
disrespected,
live in fear"

"For I'm all woman
as strong willed as he
and from this moment
the buck stops here"

Lost in You

Watching you
from up on high
Visualizing you in my mind
watching me
as I enter you

A sprite's smile
crosses you lips
your eyes roll back
under half closed lids

Sensing your sensation
at your urging of "deeper"
my engorged shaft pulsating
from hilt to throbbing tip
Pushes gently
slowly rolling back
major and minor
swollen lips

Sweet fragranced musk
permeates your opening
which closes tight
around my white hot tusk
Grasping and swallowing
from head to base
leaving, not a trace

Coaxing me in fully
you raise your hips up
drawing heels to you
with upturned hands cupped

Forming two triangles
for our support
Readied for riding
this moment's part
of our afternoon's
love sport

A sideway glance
first one,
then the other
Together we stare
at the mirror's imaged pair
One mounted, twirling
swirling
One writhing
a plunging motion
Two bodies in sync
enjoying lust's
homemade potion

We smile to each other
reversed images show
Other worldly
watching two people coupled
Two we don't yet know

Taking your legs
into my hands
Now they rest,
draped over my shoulders
Grasping your hips,
locking them with my wrists

Lifting to impale you
upon a spike
of eruption's flow
Friction sparking
love's amber glow

Faster,
wet heat surging
bodies' lubricants spill over us
with each of your heightened
downward thrusts

Emanating circle of fire
your hard clitoral button
refuses to tire
Partly hooded
Partly exposed
Kissing my thumb
and forefinger
rubbing, pinching
massaging,
as your moanings linger

"Fill me"
you cry out,
"Give me cock
fill me,
my mouth
my ass
my breasts,
I'm your whore
your pussy galore"

"Rub your cock and balls
all over my body
In and out
Up and down
here, there, all around"

"Penetrate me
everywhere
you dare
For I am yours
at this moment,
no matter the cost'

Ecstasy explosion
Mental erosion
Emotional corrosion
In each other
we are lost

Magnificent Mind

As extraordinary
as the mind is,
its functions immense
capabilities and speed
often times unmatched
you, your body
may be totally taxed
while you, your mind
never needs to rest

You, your mind never sleeps
even when you, your body does
because you, your mind
is actually you, your thoughts
and you, your thoughts
are applied mental energy
seeking goals
set by you,
your awakened soul

You, your soul
is where you, your spirit resides
as you, your body
continues to grow old
preparing to die

You, your soul became existent
at a moment in the past
And as such
you, the miracle
is designed to last

Until the end
and far beyond,
beyond imagination
Eternally past separation points
of origination and extinction
You, your spirit
is you, your life giving force
A cosmic universal energy
on this particular course

You, your experiences
are part of events
within this physical reality
Occupying a minute presence
purposed to allow
you, your being
to interact
with all that is here
and do your utmost best

As you, your body
restores itself through sleep
each and every day
you, your thought filled energy
never needs to rest

Mute Blind Spot

At the cocktail party
taking separate leave
for relief
Together at the urinals
three of them stood

The blind drunk,
his seeing eye dog, Spot
And one spot away
the mute
who spoke with his hand,
fingering
for conversation sake
to the blind man

Spot
watching this initial signal
alerted his master to the fact
another was there
next to the pair

The blind man heard and knew
he was not alone
"Good evening" he said
"How are you?"

-Silence, no reply-

The blind man asked
"Are you sightless also?"

"No" the mute man signed

"Guess he can't see us either Spot
Let's go"

"Good night"
gestured the mute man

New Habit

Past times
equally as foolish
On par with others
behavior inane

Immaturity today
publicly strewn,
No recall
No none
of being so
habitually rude

Played the fool
Occasionally cruel
More often than ought
degrees of crude

Thinking back
on those she knew
None, no not one
so habitually rude

Auto response today
"yea"
Ingrained until learned
uninterrupted flows
of streaming expressions
and indignant spurn

Short fuses abide
born of bravado's
desire and pride

Know it all,
with cyber access
to the rest

Time so valuable
too much to kill
idle hands, minds
Temptation's playground
turbulence filled

Actions and words
Victory's laurel to win
Barbs, Retorts
Digs to perfect
Inexcusable excuses
Ploys to erect

Continued presence
on a world's spot lit stage
Hitting the mark true
Striving to become
more habitually rude

New Now

For the Christian
who claims
now the Word to know
and new found righteousness
to the world
now to show
For the Born Again now
a new path to tread
For he and her
with new ecclesiastic pronouncements
now filling their heads

His challenge new, now proclaimed;

For the Christian
now to start
Revealed to the Christian's
understanding new heart
His followers now new
daily chore,
"Go, and sin no more"

One Foot in Front of the Other

The future uncertain
'tis nature of the beast
Producing apprehension
a little too much
to say the least
A myriad of unknowns
Possibilities which to fend
the truth is;
remain or not,
you can never go back again

The past appears seamless
ne'er wrinkle nor crease
Memories healed over
like hardened scar tissue
atop a wound,
out of sight
out of mind
a calm as peaceful
as an early morn in June

Hairline cracks of stress
remain down deep
refuse to completely mend,
the truth is;
realized or not
you can never go back again

Life in the present
Existence one day at a time
surviving this twenty four hours
juggling memories
and anticipation

One foot in front of the other
as child, teen, adult and senior
Moments parade by
in each and every relation

Searching for pastures
a little greener
Recalling only
pleasant thoughts
those labeled, 'good old days'

A facsimile to tomorrow
we would like to send
but always
in tomorrow's truth
soon it's found out
you can never go back again

Parallel

The only difference
between many poets
and internet bloggers is,
the bloggers haven't realized
to ascribe to themselves
the title, Poet

Plastic Man

'Look at me'
'Look at me'
Until it's time
for responsibility
Then wagging fingers
point somewhere else
To scapegoats
waiting in their pens;
Spouses, Strangers
Families, Friends

A lifetime spent
being deliciously cool
ostensibly, no fear
Bravados abound
a slight chance however,
let's be perfectly clear
When accountability's
hydra heads appear
and their trumpets' echoes
resound
Excuses arise from confrontations
flanks and rear

Investments made
In the spotlight to remain
Flash over substance
the name of this game
Pseudo intellect
Education? No Need!

Info influences arrive
via pop culture magazines
announcing self-idolatry proclamations
"What more does it take
for the world to see
the object of my attention
resides in the mirror's
glorious me"

No reason
No need
to grow or change
from the comfort zone
of pubescence range

Rainbow Ends

Morning's greeting
Prism of light
Experienced by one
Seen by others, competing?

This place
This time
Doors open wide
windows too
to the stars
unto the horizon
and now there are two

Echoes of love
in spectral glory
Tunnel of light
diffusely freed . . .

Pots of gold
at each rainbow's end
Love filled compassion
or
Illusions of greed?

Red Robin Hood

Little Red Robin
peeking from beneath her hood
Wishes she might
Hopes she could

Wandering Wolf
smiling ear to ear
"Come closer my dear,
You have nothing to fear"

"But you Sir,
dressed in sheep's garb,
you make it difficult
you make it hard"

Flashing dagger sharp teeth
"Be assured
through and through
yes,
it is hard for you"

"Shall I stay the course
on this path?
Or join you Wolf
in blissful gaff?"

"Whatever you want
sweet, sweet Red
I'm counting on you
to use your head"

"I would love to
be with you
to be caressed
and shown
But my father's mother said
'come straight home' "

"No need Red
to listen to Him
to her
or anyone of them
Somehow we'll get through
just me, just you

For as you must
already know
I am of that other world
The one into which
you desire to go
It is my job
my duty
my task,
to do whatever
you might ask

Your desires and wishes and wants
await
There,
beyond yonder gate
Join me Red
Here,
take my arm
Together we'll stroll
no need for alarm

Through this hallowed gate
is your new world
your new life
your new fate

Look up,
down our new stretch of road
Prepare yourself Red
to take on my load

See here from behind us
comes now the fact
the arrival,
the hungered,
the rest of my pack

Know it
Believe it
For now it is true
My world gives you
your covets,
your desires,
all is for you

You asked for a treat
Now run
or lie down
So we may eat

Through and through
what I want
what was planned
all I intended to do,
is simply and totally
devour you"

Red of the Hood
Who wished she might
Who hoped she could

Rest in Peace

Every person who lives
leaves behind an impression
One on exhibit
to others who are left
Etched on a headstone
or scribed in an obit

Restful Season

If you don't want to be here
then be somewhere else
Quit pretending
you have a valid reason
to put us through
another season,
of you
and your painstaking
self pity

If you don't want to be here
then be somewhere else
Stop peddling
what you believe
are pertinent excuses
designed to drag us down
through another season
of your inane
moaning and groaning

If you don't want to be here
then be somewhere else
Life is too short
to hear you whine,
over how difficult it is
for you to get out of bed
and bless us
with another season
of your presence

If you don't want to be here
then be somewhere else
You made a choice
to here spend this season
whatever your reason
Now do us and yourself
a favor of grace
and be next season
some other place

Sex Sells

Decked out,
dressed to the nines
Now, no longer confined

In a past perceived
as a living hell
Now to discover
if sex really sells

Time to penetrate
the bond tightly bound
between these three
Time to find out single handedly
where fun and fame and fortune be found

Peahen parading
pretentious prance
Questing a colorful
preening new mate
with whom to dance
Not at heaven's Pearly
but at gold's gilded gates

Head held high
Back is straight
Bust protrudes suggestively
Flag is up
Game of coy is on
Goal to become
a local celebrity

It's about the money,
then the fun
Becoming known
as number one
Learn to put aside
the guilt, the shame
It's all for money's
salacious ride
on the coat-tails of
new found fame

Attention disorder
was her plea
"All attention
must be on me"
Not a true 'gold digger'
as one might say
But the notches on her bed posts
did convey
the fun, fame and fortune
she craved

Slave to Fashion

Pigeon toed from birth
fallen arches and ingrown toenails
suffered on both feet
Skin so rough it aches
bleeds, chaff's and peels
Strained calf muscles fallen below
two arthritic knees
yet there she is hobbling,
on five inch platform heels

Thirty pounds overweight
that much she'll admit
Fleshy rolls, one and two
now visible front and back
"Clingy is the style" she quips
Wonder when it was
she last checked
those seams with fabric rips

Her skirts,
"not too short" she states
By standards today, no risk
Of course she can't sit down
except behind her desk

Her choice in length
designed to please
making male eyebrows rise
Except drawn to those
are ripples and pits
bespeckling the backs
of her cottage cheese thighs

She states she's stylish today
Feeling as if in heaven
"I think I look pretty damn good,
for forty-seven"

"My clothing gets attention
everywhere I go
and at half the price
I've doubled my wardrobe
'cuz me and my daughter
wear the same clothes"

Starvation

Identify that which brings about sadness
therein lies the source of struggle
It is in that place
manifestations of problems are graced

The enduring myth of heaven
belies emotions and feelings so intense
the body can't contain them
The greatest gift of the universe: 'free will'
and each will choose;
how
why
and when
it is used

Synapse Interruptus

You hope it turns out to be
exactly as expected,
and so it goes
while counting down
you hope and pray
vehemently

All are God's scribes;
by who they are
by what they do

Each writes a solitary story
for others to see,
our script
our role
our reality
Written by
none other than we

All synapses firing visionarily
New paths opened
The future's touch
within your reach
What will you do
to make it true?

Taken In

Invite me in
but be forewarned
once discovered
soon will be found
a bonded acquaintance made
As with the stray
taken in
who quickly sweeps
your heart away

Plying with a verbal elixir
a Merlin's magical blend
The snake oil salesman
rambles on
through twists
and turns and bends

Questions asked
Opened doors
Desires soon be known

Full frontal assault
reality by choices,
decisions
Soon to be shown

Task Priorities

We all have priorities
motivating us
to finally move to action

For some it is
the need to be right
Others to be in control
Martyr status tickles
a few jaded senses
For a many it's in the words
"you're the best!"

It's fear of loss
for all the rest

A primary agenda needed
for many a task completed?
Make a mountain out of that mole hill
whenever they might be asked
Not as it were
in order to grow
but to stab at
jab and grasp,
that little light
at the end of the tunnel
flooding themselves with adulation
hoping somehow they might glow

Ask them a question,
"why" they ask?
"What is involved
in this particular task?"

With that we must
begin the beguine
to determine the place
they will choose to be
The true reasoning result
of their fatale accompli

"It may be too tough
I'm just not sure"

"There may not be enough time
for such a strenuous task"

"Are you sure it has to be
exactly that way?"

"This appears to be
such a daunting task"

"I'm pretty sure
it can't be done"

"There's just no way
I can promise which day
the terms of success
might finally be met"

"And the truth be told
it's not a good bet"

"But wait"

"No,
Maybe"

"No, I don't think so
or believe"
(Pause for effect)

[Want
Need
Status
Love
Fear of Loss,]
('not doing it
might cost me my job')

"Ok, I'll do it!
When do I get started?"
"I'm ready,
Put me to the test"

No need, forget it
the project's completed
and already sent by 'FedEx'

Three Year Tour

Here's a proposition
for your consideration,
say you could live
your dream
whatever it may be
You could be rich
or famous,
respected
or loved
You could excel
in any endeavor
field and occupation,
or none of the above

What if you were
independently wealthy
and could do nothing at all
except, shop or fish or play

What if you could do
anything you wanted
Would an offer such as this
be of interest to you?

As you are aware
each coin has two sides
With that in mind
what would you be willing to do
to have your dream come true?

Except,
at the end of year three
It would also be
the end of you

Would you choose your dream's
fulfilled enjoyment
if at month thirty-six,
your body be spent?
your soul be sent?

That's the choice
Jesus of Nazareth made
for himself
for you and yours
His dream to serve
His life to give up,
after His three year tour

Time

Reflection upon wasted time
pursuing lust filled desires
Pain born of expended energies
multiplied within the hours

A ray of truth
piercing dark shadows
of humiliation
Seeping through a crack
in the door of degradation
Casting an elongated spike
from here
to the horizon of eternity
After all these years hidden
Shame grows as a dank mold
upon the blot
of a stained psyche

Oh to be free
free from the grind
delayed before
now daily paid for
As if a cancer
making captive the mind

Wasted days
Wasted nights
Time, heavily invested
dedicated to the chase
Eroding prosperity
as it gnaws at
false promised tranquility

Oh to be free
free of the guilt
From a mound
stone by stone
mountainous walls have been built

Time, in blocks
freely given away

Time, appearing endless
never stolen, yet cast aside

Time, consumed by selfishness
unable now to be reclaimed

Tripping

From here
to there
to eternity,
How far exactly
would that trip be

Have we trod these paths
more than once
Many say yes
Others an emphatic NO
For a few
it's déja` vu

To travel the light fantastic
requires character of depth

Untrue
and unworthy
are three cents a copy
while originals, priceless
their value a subjective guess

You're an original
look around
not another like you to be found
You say
you want
to be a star
Understand
that's what you are

For your place
in the heavens
in this universe wide
is now guaranteed
to be on one side,
or the other

Within God's grasp
within His reach,
or separated by
gnashing teeth
For this life may be
that drop in the bucket
when compared
to your next reality

So heed
the Word well
and understand,
the truth
the choice
of a heaven
or hell,

is yours
is in your hands

Truth Serves Not Itself

There are two kinds of people
in the world
There are leaders
(This is evident by their decisions)
There are followers
(This is evident by their choices)

Followers
think they are leaders
because they follow those
they believe are leading
(This is evident by their actions)

Leaders however
are always looking
to do the opposite,
or that which is different
than followers,
in order to retain
and sustain
their role
as leader

Ultimate leaders
have a limited number of followers
For these leaders attempt
to come from truth;
in their decisions
in their choices
in their actions
in their lives,

and truth
is the one place
of moral indemnity
followers want to avoid

Wave Rider

Skimming the water's surface
against the drag
of the skeg
In the bask
of an eastern rising sun
An increasing swell
catches body and board,
the next ride
has begun

With the slightest of perceivable jerks
the power of propulsion
is transferred from arms and hands
back to nature

Remaining motionless
without standing
the board now a surface glider
becomes one with the wave
running silently above the outstretched calm

A sensation of low level flight
the wave rider
now a seabird,
inches above the water line

Standing, one experiences momentarily
a euphoric mastery over the water,
and then
a sense of acknowledgment
to the unknown mysteries
held secreted in its depths

Quickly evident
is the immense force and inertia
behind and beneath the board
As speed increases
ambient wind resistance is felt,
then suddenly acute awareness
of a turbulent cresting power
off the rear flank

A scene of churning white water
born of the breaking wave
mixes and thrashes in agitation
with only one goal and desire
to overtake and consume,
the wave rider

Plunging the rider
into its tumultuous existence
will serve to prove once again
or perhaps
once and for all
which is eternal,
the ocean's swelling permanency
and which is temporal,
the riding visitor

When In . . . Jr. High

What started out
as liberation
founded in the past
Those in the '40's
imagined mistakenly
somehow it would last

In the world of sports
when did doing what
you're paid to do
merit showing off
and acting as if
you were the first ever
to catch a pass,
hit the ball
out of the park,
make a basket
or score a goal
as seconds on the scoreboard
continue to unfold?

Why do you think
you're paid those big bucks
simply, for showing up?
We hate to burst
your self-aggrandizing bubble
you're not in Tiger's league yet,
chump

When did aberrant
and egotistical behavior
become a blooming bud?

What started out
as acknowledgment
of a growing smaller world
and planet of men
Those in the '50's
after a world war
envisioned communal amends

In the world of popularity
when did it mean
not giving your best
to honor the audience in attendance
When did we lose the critics' muse
as an opportunity
to flourish, grow
and improve

When did aberrant
and egotistical behavior
become common place?

A changing
of the guard
those in the '60's
took to the street
and campus yard

In the world of education
when did being there
give license to
inconsiderate
disrespectful
and blatantly rude behavior
towards peers
instructors
and the institution itself?

When did aberrant
and egotistical behavior
become acceptable?

Mutating out of a
brotherhood philosophy
Those in the '70's
planted seeds
of personal absurdity

In the world of work
when did arriving armed
with litanies of excuse
become acceptable
to be proffered
as a daily ruse,
for irresponsibility

When did aberrant
and egotistical behavior
become glorified?

The '80's started and ended
with "I'm 'OK', you're a jerk"
evidence it was destined
never to work

In the world of entertainment
when did paying your dues
equate to not learning your craft
remembering the lyrics
or even carrying a tune?

When did aberrant
and egotistical behavior
become accepted as the norm?

The '90's were
"all about me"
filling our needs
with illusions of greed

Generations living
within each empire's history
discover for themselves
there's no hidden mystery
to life's lesson core,
being a part
of the brotherhood of man
is ultimately more

When did aberrant
and egotistical behavior
become our way of life?

A new millennium this century
named and called twenty-first
arrives with a gluttonous quest
to quench an arid thirst
of 'I only do
what I want and choose'

Those of these new years
Two thousand plus
snared by a trap
where evil perpetuates
in all possible ways
and over-exposed by every medium
attitudes, beliefs
and perceptions assured
"Not only can I do
whatever I want
I'll do it with reckless abandon
and an 'in your face'
'try to top that' hauteur"

Empires of the past
each were brought to their knees
and eventually ground into oblivion,
and so it will be
with this society of ours
the one in which
we currently reside

When did aberrant
and egotistical behavior
become our placard of pride?

XXX

Cyber sex is my life
It's even better
than doing my wife

All designed
for my release
It's better than living
in ancient Greece

Anything goes
on my computer screen
The women even smile
as I make them scream

Most sites
want to charge a fee
but I searched and searched
and found one that was free

Of course there's no hard core
except for the teasers
They've convinced me all women
are just male pleasers

There's bondage, domination
lots of S & M
On top
On bottom
Her with her
and him with him
Their carnal knowledge
makes my heart and heads spin

The mind is a wonderfully curious thing
it makes me forget about the ring
The one on my finger
which once meant so much
Now I revel
in more and more smut

I'm really ok
I'm not at all ill
I take lots of pills
and watch Dr. Phil

And Oprah
MoPo
Rikki
Montel,
and just for fun
Springer, late night
what the hell

Sure,
I've put some distance
between me and my family
But it's an I
Me
My world
and I live it happily

I just stop in to see
all my favorite
XXX's
That's where my mind and body
meet at their nexus

My family waits
for me to come round
To be husband and father
brother and son
But I'd rather have
my cyber fun

Remember,
"it's all about me"
I even bought the T-shirt
for all to see

I'd rather have it my way
and continue to whine
Than admit I could kick
this lifestyle habit
of mine

I'm not responsible
for all I do,
I don't even
have a clue
I'm the victim here,
Don't you see that?
I've exchanged all values
for a cyber trap

So when I am old
lonely
and put away
I can look back,
back on the days
Days I spent drowning
in cyber sex, sex, sex, sex
And blame someone else
for my ruined life's hex . . .

For to stop all this cybering
and avoid it's snare
I would have to not hit
the keyboard keys,
that take me there

Other books by Branch Isole

REFLECTIONS ON CHROME ©
Parking Lot Confessions in Poetic Prose
ISBN 0-9747692-5-8

SEEDS OF MANA'O ©
Thoughts, Ideas and Opinions in Poetic Prose
ISBN 0-9747692-1-5

BARKING GECKOS ©
Stories and Observations in Poetic Prose
ISBN 0-9747692-2-3

God. . .i believe ©
Simple Steps on the Path of Spiritual
Christianity ™
ISBN 0-9747692-0-7

Order books by Branch Isole at
www.manaopublishing.com
Questions, Comments; go to our website
and click on the 'contact' link.

Living on the island of Maui, Branch Isole is the 'voyeuristic poet' who shares Mana'o* and God's Word in writing and with individuals and groups visiting Hawaii.

Branch also writes poetry, articles and short stories for journals, magazines, newsletters and on the internet at www.manaopublishing.com

*Mana'o (pronounced Ma Na O) is Hawaiian for 'Thoughts, Ideas and Opinions'.